Wild About Wheels

AMBULANCES

by Keli Sipperley

PEBBLE
a capstone imprint

Pebble Emerge is published by Pebble, an imprint of Capstone.
1710 Roe Crest Drive
North Mankato, Minnesota 56003
www.capstonepub.com

Library of Congress Cataloging-in-Publication Data
Names: Sipperley, Keli, author.
Title: Ambulances / by Keli Sipperley.
Description: North Mankato, Minnesota : Pebble, [2022] | Series:
Wild about wheels | Includes bibliographical references and index. |
Audience: Ages 6–8. | Audience: Grades 2–3. | Summary: "A person needs
to get a hospital quick! What vehicle can get them there fast? An
ambulance! Ambulances carry the equipment needed to help people in an
emergency. Young readers will find out about ambulances, their main
parts, and how these important vehicles are used"—Provided by publisher.
Identifiers: LCCN 2020025516 (print) | LCCN 2020025517 (ebook) |
  ISBN 9781977132314 (library binding) | ISBN 9781977133250 (paperback) |
  ISBN 9781977153791 (ebook pdf)
Subjects: LCSH: Ambulances—Juvenile literature. | Ambulance
service—Juvenile literature.
Classification: LCC TL235.8 .S58 2021 (print) | LCC TL235.8 (ebook) | DDC
629.222/34—dc23
LC record available at https://lccn.loc.gov/2020025516
LC ebook record available at https://lccn.loc.gov/2020025517

Image Credits
Alamy: Ludmila Smite, 15; Capstone Studio: Karon Dubke, 12, 21 (art supplies); iStockphoto: FangXiaNuo, 19, HeliRy, 16, InsectWorld, 17, kali9, 6, LightFieldStudios, 11, Monkey Business Images, 7, simonkr, 8; Shutterstock: Alexander Oganezov, cover, back cover, bakdc (background), throughout, Bandersnatch, 4, michaeljung, 10, OgnjenO, 13, Pat Saza, 5, Red Orange, 21 (drawing), Tyler Olson, 9, William Perugini, 14

Editorial Credits
Editor: Amy McDonald Maranville; Designer: Cynthia Della-Rovere; Media Researcher: Eric Gohl;
Production Specialist: Katy LaVigne

Printed in the United States   4723

Table of Contents

Words in **bold** are in the glossary.

WHAT AMBULANCES DO

Ring, ring! What's your **emergency**? Help is on the way. An ambulance is coming!

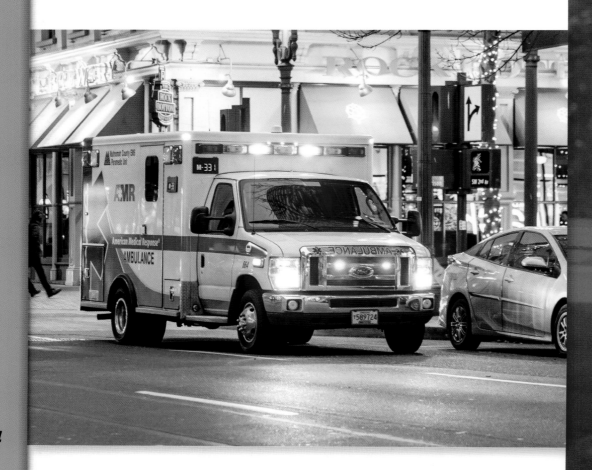

Woo, woo! A siren sounds. Red lights flash. The ambulance races down the road. Other drivers hear the sirens. They know the ambulance must hurry. The drivers get out of the way. The ambulance zooms past.

An ambulance is a vehicle that carries people who are sick or hurt. People can need help anywhere. They might be at school or work. They might be at home or in a car. An ambulance goes to the patient's location. Then the patient is rushed to a hospital.

Look Inside

Ambulance workers are trained to save lives. They care for the patient on the way to the hospital. Ambulances hold the tools they need.

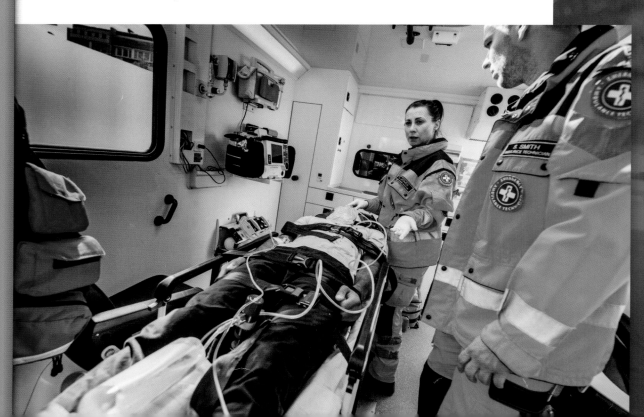

The driver sits up front in the cab. There is a two-way radio. The radio lets the ambulance workers talk to the hospital workers. Then the hospital can be ready.

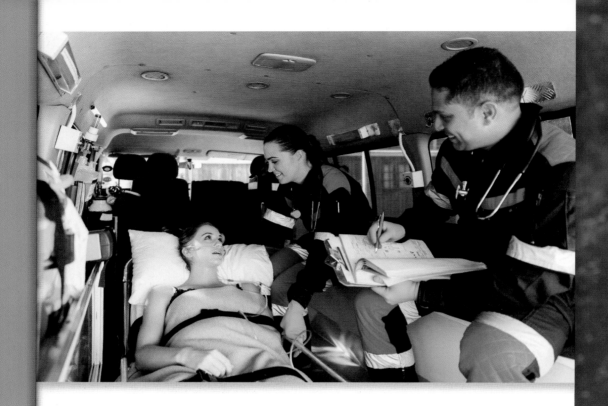

The patient lies on a stretcher. Ambulance workers strap into seats. Drawers hold medicines and bandages. Medical machines line the walls. The machines need **electricity** to work. The **engine** gives the machines electricity while the ambulance is running.

Some ambulances have **battery** units. The batteries create electricity. This electricity powers the machines while the ambulance's engine is off.

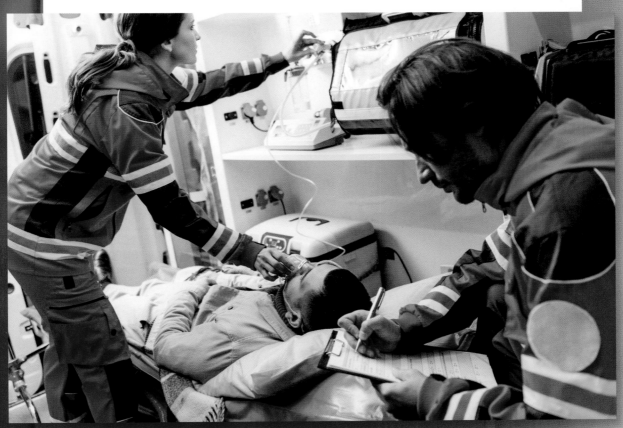

Look Outside

Ambulances can be different sizes. Some are small. They look like vans. Others are bigger. They look like trucks.

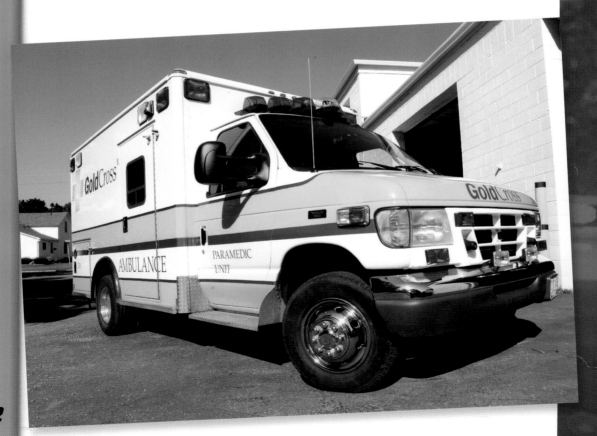

Star of Life symbol

Ambulances have colored lights and sirens on top. The lights and sirens let people know that there is an emergency.

All ambulances have a **symbol** on the outside. The symbol is called the "Star of Life." It tells people the ambulance is a medical vehicle.

Some ambulances can be raised and lowered with the push of a button. This helps workers get patients in and out easily.

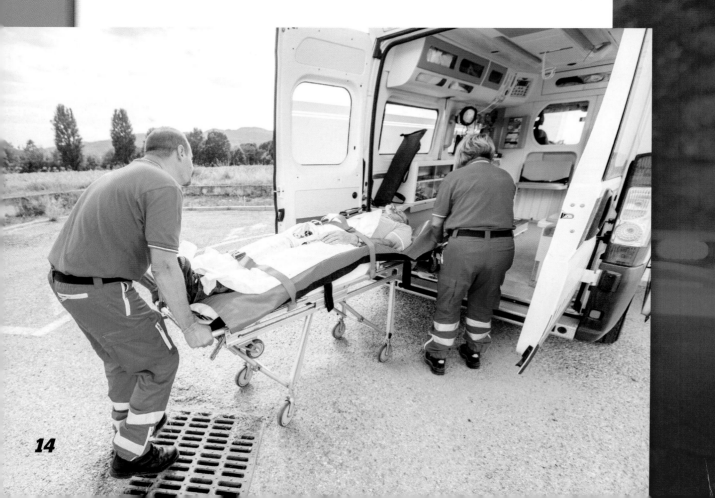

Many roads are bumpy. But the ambulance hardly bounces! It has strong **shock absorbers**. The shock absorbers help make the ride smooth. It's important to keep a hurt person from being bounced around too much.

Not all ambulances are on roads. Some places are surrounded by water. Some places don't have safe roads. Helicopter, airplane, and boat ambulances come to the rescue. Ambulances travel by land, air, or water to quickly help someone in need.

AMBULANCE DIAGRAM

lights

ADVANCED LIFE SUPPORT

Star of Life symbol

RAMEDIC UNIT

cab

58

patient

stretcher

19

Design an Ambulance

If you could design an ambulance, what would it look like? Where would you put the lights? Where would you put the stretcher and the supplies? Draw the outside of your ambulance. Then draw the inside.

Glossary

battery (BA-tuh-ree)—a container that stores energy; a battery can produce electricity

electricity (i-lek-TRISS-uh-tee)—energy made by the flow of charged particles

emergency (i-MUR-juhn-see)—a sudden, dangerous situation that requires immediate action

engine (EN-juhn)—a machine that uses fuel to power a vehicle

shock absorber (SHAHK ab-ZORB-ur)—a device for softening jolts and vibrations

symbol (SIM-buhl)—a design or object that stands for or represents something else

Read More

Abbot, Henry. *I Want to Drive an Ambulance.* New York: PowerKids Press, 2017.

Schuh, Mari C. *Rescue Vehicles.* North Mankato, MN: Pebble, a Capstone imprint, 2019.

Internet Sites

Ambulance Facts for Kids
kids.kiddle.co/Ambulance

Fun Kids Live: Paramedics-Ambulance
www.funkidslive.com/learn/hallux/map-of-medicine/paramedics-ambulance/

Index